Endorsements

My good friend Dan Kreft has written a series of books dealing with Christian apologetics for middle-school-aged children and their parents. I believe that children, parents, ministers, missionaries, public school teachers and Sunday school teachers can and will benefit from this material if they are willing to invest the time to work through it. I picked it up thinking I was going to be reading a simplistic primer for children, but this is actually a crossover book that is going to benefit children and adults. It takes a very good writer to pull this off, and Dan has done it. He asks hard questions in a surprisingly provocative manner and provides straightforward and transferable answers. He sorts and separates fact from fiction and biblical teaching from religious folklore. Buy these books, read these books, and put this material to work helping you, your family, and others navigate the troubled waters of atheistic secularism and religious compromise that are pulling so many Christian children and families under their pounding waves.

— KARL I. PAYNE,
author of *Spiritual Warfare* and the
Transferable Cross Training series

I truly enjoyed reading "Jesus" Is Not the Answer to Every Sunday School Question. *I was fascinated as Dan recounted each lesson, the questions his students asked, and the terrific responses he offered to them. Dan is obviously a gifted apologist, and this well-written introduction to apologetics and theology offers a lot for people to learn from.*

– JASON CARLSON,
President, Christian Ministries International

This is a "must-read" for those confronting the challenges of the world, defending our faith against Mormons and putting the Jehovah Witnesses in their proper theological place.

— BRITT BEEMER,
CEO of America's Research Group
and coauthor of *Already Gone*

"Jesus" Is Not the Answer to Every Sunday School Question sets the foundations of Christian doctrine and theology solidly on the infallible Scriptures and on the nature of the one true God. It seeks to do so in a way that would be winsome to young people, who desperately need the truths taught in it.

— JAMES B. NANCE,
author of logic and rhetoric curricula

I greatly enjoyed reading through Dan Kreft's "Jesus" Is Not the Answer to Every Sunday School Question series. He's intentionally gathered flowers from the gardens of various apologists and theologians then carefully assembled them into a unique bouquet that he's gifted to the church. Dan has the ability to cull from the best Christian thinkers, tailor their message to meet the needs of Sunday school teachers and students alike, all while infusing his writing with the wit and whimsy he's known for in the classroom. If you've ever wanted material to help train your children or if you've been searching for new curriculum to use in a Sunday School setting, you needn't look any further—"Jesus" Is Not the Answer to Every Sunday School Question is probably it.

— JAMES HANSEN,
Lead Pastor, Montage Bible Church

Ostensibly a series of books for parents of preteens or their Sunday school teachers, in reality they demand a much larger audience. All Christians young and old, with or without kids of their own, will find them of great value to help solidify their own faith and better arm themselves in defense and witness thereof. Each of my two children completed Dan's sixth-grade class, and it was my pleasure to read his weekly emails and even sit in on several of the classes. Not only did my kids learn and grow from the class, but so did I. Dan's material is well-researched and informative and presented in a way that is not only challenging but also an enjoyable read.

— BOB ELLIOT

These books definitely need to be on the shelf of anybody who wants to strengthen his knowledge of the Bible and fulfill 2 Timothy 3:16, 17! It's written perfectly so all ages can understand and learn. Plus, it gives you a few good laughs along the way.

— ELLY W.,
former student

Dan's books aren't nearly as good as mine, but they're still pretty good. You should read them.

— JESUS

"JESUS" IS N0T THE ANSWER TO EVRY SUNDAY SCHOL QUESTION

BOOK 2: WHO IS GOD?

DAN KREFT

"Jesus" is Not the Answer to Every Sundy School Question
Book 2: Who Is God? Copyright © 2018 by Daniel L. Kreft

ISBN 978-1-7327592-1-3

Cover design by Avery Hutcherson
Illustrations by Caleb A. Kreft
Editing and page formatting by ChristianEditingServices.com

In loving memory of Dr. Ken Hutcherson, who discipled me for twelve years and whose voice I hear on nearly every page of this book.

Luke 6:40

Contents

Foreword

We have all seen the research: about two-thirds of teenage evangelical Christians lose their faith during their first year of college. Young people growing up in Christian homes and attending Bible-believing churches are not being adequately trained to defend and sustain their faith during their college years. Obviously something is terribly wrong. Various solutions to this problem have been proposed. But at this time nothing seems to be working.

One thing many Christian leaders fail to realize is this: a person cannot lose something he never had. We incorrectly assume that merely because teenagers have attended church, youth group, and Sunday school and make a profession of faith that they are actually saved. We assume, often without any good evidence, that a teenager is a genuine believer. Unfortunately, so little truly biblical preaching and teaching are taking place in evangelical churches today that it is not safe to presuppose this. Just because a young person has been exposed to church, youth group, and Sunday school does not mean he is saved— even if he says all the right words. Has he been taught the essential doctrines of the Christian faith? Does he know how to defend his beliefs? Sunday school is an excellent place to provide the hands-on teaching and discipleship necessary to evangelize and disciple our youth.

This is why Dan Kreft is calling for what he refers to as a "rebooting of Sunday school." He does not believe Sunday school should be merely "fun and games." Christian youth must be taught the essential doctrines of the Christian faith—

and they must be taught how to defend those doctrines. These students must clearly understand the gospel message before they can truly trust in Jesus for salvation. And if their faith will stand against the assaults that will come in their college and adult years, they must be able to make a defense of their faith (1 Peter 3:15). Dan believes that Sunday school, properly done, can be an effective way to ground young people in the doctrines of the faith and equip them to withstand the anti-Christian attacks they will face in their adult years.

Imagine a Sunday school class where students are actually required to do homework! Imagine a Sunday school class where students are taught evidences for the Bible being God's Word, solid reasons to believe that God created the universe, and proofs that Jesus bodily rose from the dead. This is just a glimpse into the type of Sunday school that Dan teaches. And he wants to help other Christian Sunday school teachers do the same.

Dan has developed a Sunday school curriculum in which students learn about the attributes of God, the doctrine of the Trinity, and the doctrine of the Bible. This curriculum discusses the biblical teaching about creation and why it is important. Other topics include Noah's Ark and the global flood, a defense of the resurrection of Jesus, and the person of Christ.

Dan also takes time to refute non-Christian belief systems like the Latter-day Saints (Mormons) and the Jehovah's Witnesses. Finally, this work closes with explaining why Jesus of Nazareth is unique among all humans.

Dan wants churches to take Sunday school much more seriously. It is a powerful instrument that the evangelical church can use to genuinely lead their youth to Christ's salvation and help them to grow in their faith. In a culture that no longer loves Jesus, this book should be in the library of every Christian leader. Churches, Sunday schools, Christian schools, and home school families will benefit greatly from reading this book and applying the valuable truths contained within its pages. The youth of the church are the future of the church. It is time to get serious about training our young people to "contend earnestly for the faith which was once for all handed down to the saints" (Jude 3). Now is the time for church leaders to stand up and train our youth in the whole counsel of God. In my humble opinion, this book is an excellent resource to enable the church to take that stand.

— DR. PHIL FERNANDES

Pastor of Trinity Bible Fellowship, Bremerton, Washington President of the Institute of Biblical Defense Apologetics and Philosophy Instructor (Crosspoint Academy, Shepherds' Bible College, Columbia Evangelical Seminary)

Thank You

Adrienne Burton, my mother-in-law, put the idea of turning my weekly update emails into a book. Without her gentle insistence, this series would never have been written.

Haakon Sorenson, Mary Lynn Spear, Bob Elliot, and Karl Payne, who were all generous with their time, sharp eyes, red pens, and challenging questions.

Kathy Holland, my ninth-grade English teacher, wrote on one of my papers that she hoped to see my work in print someday. Her persistent admonitions to "show, don't tell" still ring in my ears after 30 years.

And, of course, my bride, Adair, who has walked with me through the emotional rollercoaster ride of writing my first book, who patiently endured stacks of books piled up where they don't belong and helped me find the time to work on it. In you I truly have found what is good and have received favor from the LORD (Proverbs 18:22).

The Story Behind This Series

Over a decade ago I was told by the junior high youth pastor that most of the kids that matriculated into his program every year had no idea what they believed or why, and he asked if I would be willing to teach the kids the fundamentals of the faith—something I was eager to do. So I was paired with an experienced schoolteacher, and off we went on our mission to prepare the kids not only for junior high but also for life beyond the church walls.

The first thing we did together was to completely abandon the elementary school curriculum that the rest of the Sunday school classes were using as both of us found it thoroughly uninspiring. So we set off to write our own from scratch. Over the course of the next couple of years we would make revisions, but the basic lessons never changed, and the same lessons were taught for the next five years or so. It was a formula that seemed to work: the kids were having fun, the teachers were having fun, the parents weren't complaining, so we figured we had a pretty good thing going—that is, until two events turned everything completely upside down.

The first event was my co-teacher announcing that she felt led to other ministries at the church (she had been teaching a *very* long time); I was going to be on my own in the lead for the first time ever. The ante had been upped.

The second concurrent event was reading *Already Gone*, by Ken Ham and Britt Beemer, which analyzes and discusses the results of a survey made of 1,000 individuals between the ages of 20 and 30 who once attended conservative, evangelical churches every week or nearly every week when growing up but never or rarely attend today.[1] Pollster George Barna had already documented that six out of ten 20-somethings who had attended church during their teen years were "already gone," having abandoned their faith.[2] Ham and Beemer, however, wanted to find out why. In a nutshell, this is what they found:

1.   Kids who attended church and Sunday school *regularly* and *faithfully* while growing up are actually **more** likely to "bolt" than kids who do not attend as regularly;[3]

2.   Kids are being taught that various aspects of Darwinian evolution (e.g., millions of years, and even evolution itself) can be reconciled with Scripture;[4] and

3.   Sunday school teachers tend to be heavy on doctrine and "stories" but are failing to equip children to cope with the world's attacks (i.e., apologetics).[5]

They had me at the first point. The Holy Spirit reached up out of that book, slapped me across the face, and asked, "You

---

1   Ken Ham and Britt Beemer, *Already Gone* (Green Forest, AR: Master Books, 2009), 27.

2   Ibid., 23.

3   Ibid., 38–40.

4   Ibid., 49.

5   Ibid.

are a Sunday school teacher; are you part of the solution or are you part of the problem?" I've never had the problem of trying to mix the oil and water of secular theory and biblical truth, so that wasn't an issue. But the third point hit closer to home.

All the lessons I had authored and taught for the previous seven years had a smattering of apologetics in them, but nothing focused—nothing intentional. It was all just a sort of "Oh, by the way, this is what people from this other religion believe." It was informational apologetics—more trivia than substance. And what's worse, I never really *challenged* the kids in their faith and made them think. I did all the thinking and talking, and they did the listening. Isn't that the way a class is supposed to operate? Not if the results of this survey are to be believed.

I finished *Already Gone* on a Friday. Saturday night I sat down to review the next lesson, and as I read the title and the summary, a pit formed in my stomach. The next lesson was the theological equivalent of a Twinkie—a sugary snack that offers a quick "fix" but has no lasting benefit. I knew I couldn't teach it, but after just having taught a multi-week series on theology proper, I had completely run out of material. I had nothing. But as it turns out, when we come to the end of ourselves is always when God does His best work.[6] I prayed hard that night and the next morning. When the students arrived I showed them the lesson, told them why I wasn't going to teach it, closed the folder, and said, "Now what do *you* want to talk about?"

---

6   2 Corinthians 12:9.

I spent the remainder of the class answering questions that the Lord had put on their hearts. As the class came to a close, one of my six students asked me a question that I felt was too good and too deep for a 30-second sound-bite answer. So I directed the kids to take the question home, discuss it with their parents, have them sign it, and bring the answers written on paper the next week so we could discuss them. I was so excited about this new direction that on Monday night I sent an email to the parents that told them all about what had happened Sunday morning and informed them of the homework assignment expected of their children.

For the remainder of the year I never knew what I was going to teach from one week to the next, which was all at once nerve-wracking and exhilarating. What I taught from week to week was completely directed by the Holy Spirit as He laid questions on the hearts of my six students and I answered them. To paraphrase Henry Blackaby in *Experiencing God*, I simply asked God to show me where He was at work and let me join in.

What follows in this book is an edited collection of the emails I have sent to my students' parents every Monday night for the past five years, beginning with a brief letter of introduction that explains my unconventional approach to Sunday school. My prayer is that in reading these emails you will see that Sunday school can be intellectually challenging, engaging, and equipping as well as fun and that it will inspire you to step outside the box as you seek to teach the young ones under your care how to contend earnestly for the faith that was once for all entrusted to the saints (Jude 3).

The Attributes of God

Part 1: Eternal, Omnipresent

THIS WEEK WE STARTED A SERIES ON theology proper. Since it's good to know what we're talking about before we start talking, I first defined theology. *Theology* comes from two Greek words: θεός (*theos*), meaning "god,"[1] and λόγος (*logos*), meaning "word," "speech," "knowledge," or "discourse."[2] So theology is quite literally "knowledge of God" or more commonly "the study of God." Theology *proper* is a subset of systematic theology that concerns itself solely with the being, attributes, and work of God, which is where we'll spend the next several weeks.

---

1   Entry for Strong's #2316 - θεός, accessed August 23, 2016,
    http://www.studylight.org/lexicons/greek/gwview.cgi?n=2316.

2   Entry for Strong's #3056 - λόγος, accessed August 23, 2016,
    http://www.studylight.org/lexicons/greek/gwview.cgi?n=3056.

"So why," one might ask, "do we need to concern ourselves with theology? Is theology *really* important for me?" In a word, yes. Theology is crucial. To illustrate why, consider a typical Craigslist transaction.

BUFORD AND RUFUS

Buford posts an ad saying he wants to sell something. Rufus sees the ad and sends Buford an email saying, "I'll take it." The two make arrangements to meet at the local grocery store, but there's a problem they have to overcome—neither has ever met the other. So what is Rufus supposed to do, walk around the store all night asking everyone he meets, "Hey, are you Buford?" Of course not—the two exchange information about each other ahead of time. Rufus tells Buford, "I'll be wearing a bright orange hunter's cap," and Buford tells Rufus that he'll be wearing a ten-gallon cowboy hat with blinking lights on it. When the two get within range of one another, they'll recognize each other easily—the uncertainty of their respective identities will all but disappear. Of course, there's always the possibility that other people are wearing orange hunter's caps or ten-gallon hats trimmed with blinking lights, so that's why when they meet each other they verify their assumptions:

"Buford?"

"Yup. Rufus?"

"Yup."

And the transaction proceeds.

Hopefully the connection between this scenario and theology is obvious. As Hank Hanegraaff is fond of saying (and I'm fond of quoting), "Virtually every theological heresy begins with a misconception of the nature of God." If we do not have a proper understanding of who God is, then we will never be able to be certain that the god we're following is *the* God, and if we don't know God well, then we won't be able to discern truth from error.

A few years back, I used to participate in an atheist-vs.-theist blog. Early on in our discussion, the other theist on the blog posted the following:

> *I believe that God is the omnipotent, omniscient creator of the universe and all that is in it. He is human in form, but timeless and conscious in a way mortal man cannot comprehend. God operates at a higher level of understanding than does man. God is also empathic and knows the full range of human emotion (having created man in his image, it stands to reason He would have created man in His likeness in other ways, too). In addition, God is omnibenevolent. All-powerful, all-knowing, all-loving. These are the traits of God.*

> *This is how I see God. He is all those "omnis" from our perspective because we just don't understand how He does it all. But as we learn the methods and elements of His ways—as we become more omniscient ourselves—this doesn't diminish who God is; it simply makes us more like Him. I believe that that is precisely God's purpose—to make us each like Him and to teach us to become gods of other universes ourselves.*[3]

3   Cory Nani, "Why I Believe…" (posted September 22, 2010), accessed August 30, 2016, http://atheistvstheistdebate.blogspot.com/2010/09/why-i-believe.html.

Can you spot the unbiblical doctrines in this quote?[4] If you can't, it's time to brush up on your theology!

We'll kick off our study of theology proper by examining some of God's attributes. In this class we'll look at seven attributes that God does not share with His creation and make mention of a handful He does share with us. This week we got around to only two of the seven:

GOD IS ETERNAL (Psalm 90:2; Isaiah 57:15a; 2 Peter 3:8)

God has no beginning and no end. This is not the same as *everlasting,* mind you— *everlastingness* means to continue on forever but says nothing about origins or beginnings (see Figure 1-1). So *eternal* is *everlasting,* but *everlasting* is not necessarily *eternal.* In mathematical terms, *everlastingness* is a subset of *eternality.*

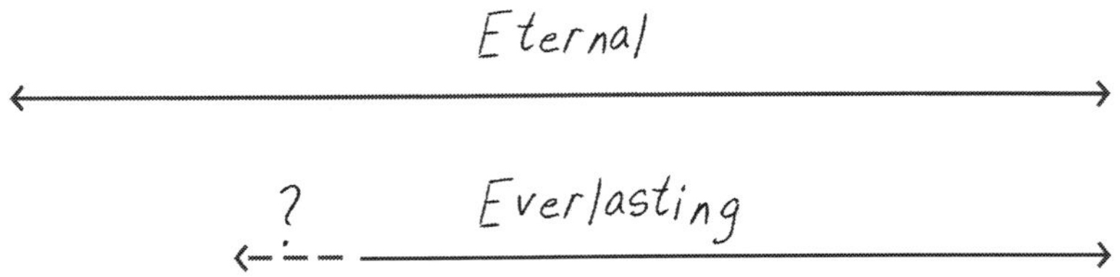

Figure 1-1

4   Some of the unbiblical phrases include "[God] is human in form" (cf. John 4:24); "He is all those 'omnis'…because we just don't understand how He does it all" —which is just another way of saying "God isn't really 'omni-anything' —we're just too dumb to 'get it,' and if we were smarter, He wouldn't seem quite so awesome"; "more omniscient ourselves" isn't necessarily unbiblical, but it is somewhat odd—like saying that a woman gets "more pregnant" every month after conception—you're either omniscient or you're not; and "teach us to become gods of other universes," which directly contradicts God's very clear declaration that there is no other god but Him. I discuss these doctrines in detail in *Book 3: Practical Apologetics.*

Why should you want an eternal God? Well, think of what it would be like if He were not eternal. If He were not eternal, that would mean that He necessarily had a beginning. Because *ex nihilo nihil fit*,[5] that would mean that Something would have had to create God. And since nothing can create something greater than itself (Romans 1:25), that Something that created God would have to be greater than God—which would make it a sort of Super God. If that's the case, then we've got the wrong God—we need to be worshiping the Über God and not the lesser deity of the Bible. This would also get us into a very nasty infinite regression.[6] But, of course, that presumes that the Über God hasn't died already, which would be a definite possibility if He were not eternal as well. So if God is not eternal, we find ourselves in the unfortunate position of possibly worshiping the wrong God as well as running the risk of being quite literally orphaned when He expires. This would be a bad thing—because it would mean that the #2 power in the universe, Satan, would be in charge.

Other than always being around, being eternal has other advantages—it means that God is not locked up in the box we call "spacetime," which brings us to our next attribute.

GOD IS OMNIPRESENT (Psalm 139:7, 8; Jeremiah 23:23, 24; Matthew 6:6)

"Om-na what? I think I get the 'present' part, but what's with this 'omni' business?"

---

5   Latin for "out of nothing nothing comes."

6   "Infinite Regression," *Conservapedia*, accessed June 24, 2016, http://www.conservapedia.com/Infinite_regression.

I'm glad you asked. The prefix *omni* comes from the Latin word *omnis*, meaning "all." So the present word (pun intended) means "all-present"—God is everywhere at once.

Why should you want an omnipresent God? You want an omnipresent God because that means that no matter where you go on this planet (or even off the planet!), you can rest assured that God is there. My brother was in Afghanistan for almost a year getting shot at on a daily basis—God was (and still is) there. I've been to Turkmenistan, Cuba, El Salvador, Latvia, and a host of other countries and, God was there too.

There's another side to this coin, though—not only does it mean that God is there to help you wherever you are, but it also means that you cannot run from Him. Jonah's malformed theology serves as an example for us today (1 Corinthians 10:1–13), that espousing a bad theology may earn you a free pass to a three-day gastric juice bath!

HOMEWORK

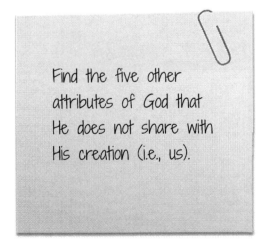

Find the five other attributes of God that He does not share with His creation (i.e., us).

The Attributes of God

*Part 2: Omniscient,
Omnipotent, Immutable*

L AST WEEK WE TALKED ABOUT GOD'S *eternality* and *omnipresence* as well as the importance of those attributes. The assignment for last week was to discover five additional attributes that God does not share with us. This week we were able to cover only three of them.

GOD IS OMNISCIENT (1 Chronicles 28:9a; Matthew 10:30; Psalm 139:2, 4; 1 John 3:20b; Ezekiel 11:5)

Again, the prefix *omni* comes from the Latin *omnis,* meaning "all," and *scient* comes from the Latin word *scientia,* meaning "knowledge." So God has all knowledge—He is all knowing. Why do you want a god who is omniscient? Well, if your god isn't all knowing, then it'd be a trivial matter to lie to him and get away with it. How many of us as parents have had to deal with scenarios like the following:

> Parent: "Who left the door open?"
>
> Offspring #1: "Not me."
>
> Offspring #2: "Not me."
>
> Offspring #3: "I didn't do it."
>
> Parent: "Well *someone* opened it and didn't close it. It sure wasn't the cats!"
>
> Offspring #1: "I dunno."
>
> Offspring #2: *shrug*
>
> Offspring #3: "I have to go potty."
>
> Parent: *facepalm*

We have some examples in Scripture that show us what to do in situations like this, but they don't always directly apply. For example, threatening to cut the door in half (per 1 Kings 3:16ff) to see which child would scream the loudest is unlikely to do anything more than grow the "honey-do" list. Thankfully, God doesn't fall for our lies, and He sees through the façades we put up.

On the other side of the coin, though, God knows when we do something for His glory when nobody else is looking, and He'll reward us accordingly. He's like Santa Claus—but with night vision goggles, GPS, Doppler radar, X-ray vision *and* ESP.

GOD IS OMNIPOTENT (John 10:28, 29; Matthew 19:26; Jeremiah 32:17, 27)

God is all-potent. *Potent* comes from the Latin *potentum*, meaning "powerful," so that makes Him all-powerful. Or as my eldest son used to say many moons ago, "Nothing is impopsicle with God!" The reason you should want an omnipotent god should be obvious: if God were not omnipotent, then it's quite conceivable that He would run into Satan in a dark alleyway somewhere, get beaten up, and have His milk money stolen from Him. Worse yet, Satan could dethrone God and take over the show. If your god isn't omnipotent, I would recommend finding a new one—unless you prefer serving a cosmic whipping boy.

GOD IS IMMUTABLE (Psalm 33:11; Malachi 3:6; James 1:17; Numbers 23:19)

God is not mutable. This does not mean, as one student suggested, that God's remote has no mute button ("I keep pressing it, but God just keeps on talking! Argh!"). Rather, it means that God is not changeable—He is the same yesterday, today, and forever (Hebrews 13:8).

Why should we want a god who is immutable? Consider what might happen if God *were* mutable: what if God decided one day that the whole "salvation by grace through faith" thing wasn't really working out so well because most cult members were living more righteous lives (at least outwardly) than those who have been redeemed by the Savior's blood? What if God decreed that salvation was going to be by works from here on out and that anyone who died before this new decree would be eternally out of luck? You want—no, you *need* an immutable God; a mutable God cannot be trusted.

Next week we'll talk about God's sovereignty. So to grease the mental skids, I present to you this week's homework.

HOMEWORK

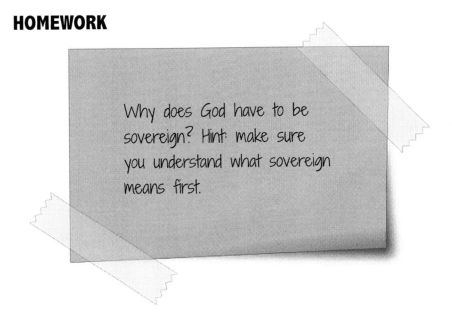

Why does God have to be sovereign? Hint: make sure you understand what sovereign means first.

The Attributes of God

Part 3: Sovereign,
Communicable Attributes

W E DID A LOT MORE REVIEW THIS WEEK OF the first five of the seven incommunicable attributes of God: eternal, omnipresent, omniscient, omnipotent, and immutable. This week we'll talk about His sovereignty.

GOD IS SOVEREIGN (Job 42:2; Ecclesiastes 7:13; Psalm 115:3; Daniel 4:35)

To be sovereign is to be in complete control, to have complete autonomy, to answer to no one.

In answer to last week's question, God *has* to be sovereign because if He weren't, then His other attributes would be rather worthless. What good is a god who is outside of space and time, has no beginning and no ending, is everywhere at once, has all knowledge, is all powerful and never changes—

yet has to get permission from someone else in order to make decisions? What good is a god whose plans can be thwarted? I submit to you that such a god would not be worth following.

God's sovereignty is without a doubt my personal favorite of His attributes. The more we understand God's sovereignty, the easier life becomes for us. This is not, of course, to say that life will be easy in the sense that we will never face any trials or tribulations or that we'll never face persecution (John 16:33), but when we understand that God is in complete control, we can rest easily knowing that *all* things work together for the good of those who love God and are called according to His purpose (Romans 8:28). Unfortunately, this has become almost cliché in Christian circles; how many of us truly believe that God is *really* in control of everything? Do we complain about "bad" circumstances? It's because we don't actually believe that God can use those circumstances for our good and His glory (Genesis 50:20)—our God is too small. Do we worry about where our next paycheck is going to come from, that we'll "run out of money before we run out of month," or how our kids are going to turn out? If so, it's because we have an underdeveloped understanding of God's sovereignty—our God is too small.

Ah, the sovereignty of God. There's nothing more reassuring to me than the knowledge that even though chaos may swirl around me, my God is neither taken by surprise nor confused about what to do—He is the immovable resting place for my soul.

SOME COMMUNICABLE ATTRIBUTES

In the final minutes of class we touched on a few attributes that God does share, at least in part, with humans: love, thankfulness, mercy, grace, wrath, jealousy.

We talked about love for a while. I asked the kids whether love ever causes pain, and one astute student went right for the quintessential example of love causing pain—the death of our Savior, Jesus Christ. It was the Father's love for us that caused Him to send His Son to die for us, and it was love that caused the Son to submit to the Father willingly, "for the joy set before Him" (Hebrews 12:2). Love is not that warm, fuzzy feeling we get inside when we see "that special person," but rather love is a decision to do what's in the best interest of the other person; it has little to nothing to do with feelings. Love has no problem causing another person pain—whether that be emotional or physical—if that pain is for the recipient's own good (e.g., corporal punishment of a wayward child, "offending" someone engaged in a sinful lifestyle, and so on).

We also talked about the difference between envy and jealousy—the former is wanting what belongs to someone else while the latter is wanting what is already yours—protecting it and guarding it from harm. Envy is *always* a sin and expressly prohibited in Scripture (Exodus 20:17), whereas jealousy is not necessarily so—after all, God is a jealous God;[1] but who hasn't shuddered at the sight of a control-freak boyfriend going ballistic should his girlfriend say hello to someone more handsome than himself?

---

1   http://www.biblegateway.com/quicksearch/?quicksearch
     =jealous+god

Next week we'll begin a multi-part series on the seventh of God's incommunicable attributes—His Tri-unity. As a warning to you and your child, the following lessons on the Trinity are the only ones that I teach that I *expect* will leave your child more confused than before we start. As a matter of fact, if the kids come out on the other side of these lessons thinking that they understand the Trinity of God *better* than they do today, then I have no doubt failed as a teacher. It's a daunting subject, but let's not let that deter us. As Obi Wan Kenobi said to Luke Skywalker as they stood on the cliff overlooking the Mos Eisley space port, "We must be cautious."[2]

HOMEWORK

> Describe the Trinity
> in your own words.
> Use analogies if you
> like, but make sure
> to use scripture to
> support your position.

---

2   *Star Wars: Episode IV--A New Hope.* Directed by George Lucas, Twentieth Century Fox Film Corporation, 1977.

The Trinity

Part 1: The "Is Nots"

IF YOU'LL RECALL FROM LAST WEEK'S update, I said that the lessons on the Trinity are the only ones I teach that I expect to confuse more than clarify—well, that is assuming I do a good job. I'm basically tasked with the impossible—explaining the Infinite using finite words and concepts crafted in a finite brain and presented to a group of children who are still learning how to think in the abstract. This makes nailing translucent, jiggly gelatinous desserts to a tree while standing on a greased pig seem easy.

When one is tasked with explaining a difficult concept to the uninitiated, a typical approach is to use an analogy or two to help ease the transition into the new topic. Take for example how electricity works. I can stand in front of a whiteboard and wax eloquent about how voltage equals current times resistance and show you how to calculate the amount of current that a circuit is going to draw, but if you've never studied electricity, you're just going to sit there and blink at me. But if I explain to you that voltage is analogous to pressure, current is the speed of the water through the pipe, and resistance to the flow of water depends upon the size, shape, and roughness of the pipe, you can form a mental image of something concrete and familiar to help you grasp the abstract concept.

Answers to last week's homework question "What is the Trinity?" were—well, interesting. As I expected, some drew pictures while some used analogies. I jokingly accused the class of cheating because quite a few of the kids cited Genesis 1:26; I'm betting those are the kids who used Google as a research tool. Just remember—if the kids write down "big words" that they've pulled directly from some website, they're going to have some 'splainin' to do.[1]

Things got *really* interesting, though, when I started playing dumb and really pressing the kids to explain their views, at times deliberately using straw man argumentation to really tie their brains into knots (it's so much fun—I can't help it!) A couple of the kids stumbled into a heresy known as modalism.[2] Another student made it sound as if the three members of the Trinity were each one-third of God, much like a pie cut into three parts. One student called the Holy Spirit an "it" and a "substance." One student would have fit in well with the Mormons when he basically said that the Trinity is

---

1   Ricky Ricardo, the Cuban co-star of the 1950s television series *I Love Lucy*, could often be heard saying this to his mischievous wife, Lucy. I used to love watching re-runs of that show when I was a kid.

2   *Wikipedia*, s.v. "Sabellianism," accessed June 28, 2016, http://en.wikipedia.org/wiki/Sabellianism.

three gods, all equal. A few students used the example of an apple (skin, flesh, seeds), and one or two particularly astute students used water in its three states as an analogy to explain the Trinity.

DESTROYING THE ANALOGIES, ONE BY ONE

Out of all the analogies I've seen applied to the Trinity, the apple is perhaps my all-time least favorite. It's a horrible example for the quite obvious reason that it doesn't have one single seed in it—it has several, which in my mind automatically queues it for rejection. A slightly better example in the same category would be the avocado or an egg as both have three clearly defined parts. But to demonstrate why they are not at all good examples, I brought in some "visual aids" for show and tell.

Eggs and avocados

Taking an egg in hand, I cracked it over a glass container and was rather dumbfounded when I saw that this jumbo ovum had not one but two yolks. Does God have a brilliant sense of humor or what? With a hearty chuckle, I asked the kids to pretend there was only a single yolk. I separated the egg into its three major parts,[3] called them by name (shell, albumen, yolk), explained what they are made of (calcium carbonate, protein, cholesterol and other fats, respectively) and asked them some questions.

Pointing at the hard, white crust I asked, "Is this 'egg'?"

---

3   Technically speaking, the egg has quite a few more than three parts: http://www.sites.ext.vt.edu/virtualfarm/poultry/poultry_eggparts.html.

"No. It's the shell."

"How about this clear, viscous fluid. Is this 'egg'?"

"No, it's 'Al Bowman' [albumen]."

"How about this yellow stuff. Is this 'egg'?"

"No, it's yolk."

A few of the kids (mostly boys—go figure) then volunteered to munch some shell and share their respective experiences with us. Unsurprisingly, all agreed that it didn't taste much like egg. I didn't go so far as to ask anyone to try the other components for fear of a parental pitchfork party.

I did the same with the avocado—cut it open and asked the same questions.

The conclusion was that the egg and avocado are thoroughly lousy analogies to use when trying to explain the Trinity because

1. Their component parts can be separated one from the other,

2. Their component parts are each made of different "stuff"—no one part by itself is equivalent in substance to the whole, and

3. The parts do not interact with each other equally (e.g., the pit touches the flesh but not the skin— unless you step on it).

Water

Water is a much better example because it doesn't suffer from the "different stuff" problem—water in each of its three states is still two hydrogen atoms bound to one oxygen atom; the only thing that changes is the velocity and spacing of the molecules. However, under ordinary conditions (standard temperature and pressure[4]) water suffers from a different problem—the three states are not coexistent. So at standard temperature and pressure this is a pretty glaring problem.

However, water is a really interesting substance. At a precise temperature and pressure, called the "triple point,"[5] water can exist in its three states at the exact same moment in time—the vapor will rise to the top of the container, below that the ice, and below that the liquid water. But even this state is problematic because if strictly applied to the Trinity, it means that while God can be Father, Son, and Holy Spirit at the *same time*, He cannot do so in the *same space* (wrap your head around *that* if you can). It also falls short because the triple point is dependent upon precisely controlled conditions for its existence, and the last time I checked, God is not a contingent being.

Musical chords

A chord in its most basic form is three or more notes played together that produce a (hopefully) pleasant sound. If we play a C, E, and G simultaneously, we get a C major chord—

---

4   *Wikipedia*, s.v. "Standard temperature and pressure," (accessed June 23, 2016), http://simple.wikipedia.org/wiki/Standard_temperature_and_pressure.

5   *Wikipedia*, s.v. "Triple point," (accessed June 23, 2016), http://en.wikipedia.org/wiki/Triple_point#Triple_point_of_water.

which sounds quite unlike the discrete notes of which it is comprised. If we listen carefully, we can still discern the individual notes that make up the chord, but when a chord is played, it becomes more than the sum of its parts. If we mute the G and play only the C and E, we no longer have a chord—we have a "major third"—which has a very different character and quality than a chord.

But the chord fails as an analogy too, because like water at its triple point, it is wholly contingent upon an external agent for its existence—the chord must be repeatedly strummed or plucked or it will decay into an empty silence.[6]

SO WHAT ANALOGY SHOULD I USE TO EXPLAIN THE TRINITY?

Ha! One might as well ask, "Which screwdriver should I use to cut this cedar tree down?" How does one explain an infinite, incomprehensible God using finite examples birthed in our Lilliputian brains? We can no more explain God than we can empty the oceans with a teaspoon. The only way to properly use an analogy to explain the Trinity is to do precisely what I've done here: lay out the analogy, explain how it represents in some small way what God is like, but then turn right back around and tear down the analogy by explaining how utterly short it falls of its goal.

---

6   This illustration appears to have been pioneered by Jeremy Begbie in *Theology, Music and Time* (Cambridge Studies in Christian Doctrine; Cambridge, England: Cambridge University Press, 2000).

WHAT'S TRUE ABOUT GOD?

Once we properly dispense with the silly notion that we can put handles on God so as to lug Him around, we then have to figure out how we're going to come to any real knowledge of who God is. So how *do* we explain the Trinity? Well, there's only one thing that's true about God: that which He tells us about Himself. It just so happens that the Bible tells us what God says about Himself, so perhaps we should start there.

HE'S NOT ME, AND VICE VERSA

It's probably safe to assume that anyone with even a passing knowledge of orthodox Christian doctrine has heard of the Trinity, and a good portion of those might even know the names of the members of the godhead: the Father, the Son, and the Holy Spirit. I drew three circles arranged in a wide triangular pattern on the whiteboard and labeled them accordingly:

Figure 4-1

I then had the kids look up and read Matthew 3:16, 17. At Christ's baptism, the Father's voice comes from the sky, the Holy Spirit descends in the form of a dove, and we find Jesus sloshing around in the muddy waters of the Jordan River. Now either Jesus is a mind-blowing ventriloquist and puppeteer, or He is not the Father and He is not the Holy Spirit.

In John 15:26 Jesus does not say that He sends Himself from Himself. That would be—weird. The Son is not the Holy Spirit, nor is He the Father. In a similar fashion, John 16:7 demonstrates unequivocally that the Son is not the Holy Spirit.

Last, in Luke 22:42 Jesus does not pray to Himself asking that He remove the cup of wrath from Himself, but rather He (the subject) makes a request of the Father (the object). The Father is not the Son.

Thus:

- The Father is not the Holy Spirit.

- The Father is not the Son.

- The Son is not the Holy Spirit.

The converses of these statements, of course, are also true: the Holy Spirit is not the Father, the Son is not the Father, and the Holy Spirit is not the Son:

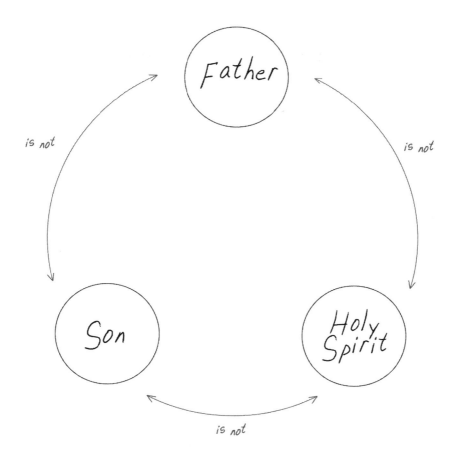

Figure 4-2

So far the Mormons, Jehovah's Witnesses, Unitarians, Oneness Pentecostals, and even Muslims are all happy and are no doubt nodding in agreement with all that has been said to this point.

AHA! SO YOU'RE A POLYTHEIST!

No, I'm not a polytheist. Don't get ahead of me. Let's go to the text.

While the Bible certainly talks about the Father, Son, and Holy Spirit in such terms as would necessitate our concluding that they are three distinct personalities, it also asserts that there is only *one* God—this we see in Deuteronomy 6:4; Isaiah 45:5, 22; 1 Corinthians 8:4–6; and James 2:19, just to name a few.

Figure 4-3

So which is it? Do we have three Gods or do we have one God? Is the Bible contradicting itself? Are Trinitarian Christians actually self-denying polytheists, as the Jehovah's Witnesses, Unitarians, Oneness Pentecostals, and Muslims assert? Stay tuned—we've got a lot more to discuss.

HOMEWORK

Trinitarians insist that Jesus is God. Does Scripture support this position? Support your answer with scripture and be prepared to defend it.

The Trinity

Part 2: The "Is's"

T HE HOMEWORK ASSIGNMENT FROM LAST week was to prove that Jesus is God.

One student cited John 11:27, wherein Martha says, "Yes, Lord; I have believed that You are the Christ, the Son of God, even He who comes into the world." This is a good verse to cite — *if* you have the right reason for citing it. Just because someone sincerely believes something, that does not make it true. For example, I can sincerely believe that I am a seven-foot-long carrot, freshly picked from the garden Sunday morning, but that doesn't make me a carrot, does it? Likewise, I could turn to one of my students and proclaim, "Thou art God!" but that doesn't make it so. Defending his answer, this student rightly stated, "This shows that Martha *believed* that Jesus is the Son of God," but there are two problems with this statement. First, it commits the fallacy of the irrelevant thesis ("true but irrelevant") since what Martha believed about Jesus is immaterial; and second, it doesn't define what "Son of God" means. If you listen to a Jehovah's Witness, he'll tell you that since a son cannot be his own father, the title "Son of God" cannot possibly mean "Jesus is God." So actually, without further clarification, which I'll provide later, this response generates more questions than answers.

Another student's answer makes me giggle: "It's as simple as John 10:30: 'I and the Father are one.'" I giggle—not because the answer is bad but because there's nothing simple about the Trinity. I love the answer for its childlike simplicity—it says to me, "Look: this is what Jesus said. It's pretty plain, isn't it? What's all the fuss about?" But unfortunately, there are many who twist Scripture into unrecognizable forms. To prepare them for this, I have to play devil's advocate. "But wait a minute," I retorted. "Last week we learned from Matthew 3:16, 17; John 15:26; and Luke 22:42 that the Father is not the Son, didn't we? You say that the Son is God, but Deuteronomy 6:4 and James 2:19 unequivocally state that there is only one God. So how in the world can the Father and the Son be 'one'?"

My retort struck its mark so I let the kids stew on the question as they sat there in shell-shocked silence. It was a beautiful thing, that silence—it's the sound of gray matter beginning to smolder. I followed up with some questions to help nudge them in the right direction, but I won't bore you with those. Suffice to say that I got them sufficiently tied in knots and then had to untie them. But before untying this knot, I wanted to talk about the other two members of the Trinity.

THE FATHER IS GOD

The statement "The Father is God" is by far the easiest to prove from Scripture, for the phrases "God our Father," "Father God," and "God the Father" are so numerous, particularly in the pages of the New Testament, that it can be difficult to find a page on which they do *not* appear. Those that we noted in class, however, were Ephesians 5:20; Isaiah 64:8; Isaiah 63:16b; 2 John 1:3; 2 Peter 1:17; 1 Peter 1:2; and Ephesians 6:23.

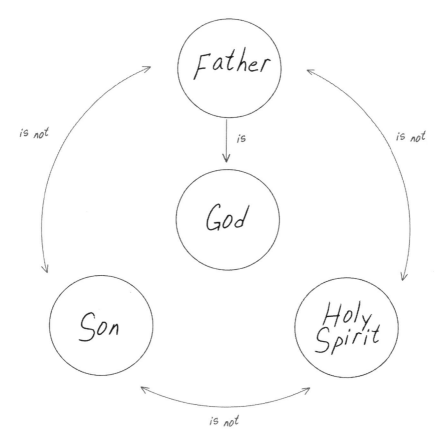

Figure 5-1

Not surprisingly, I don't think I've ever had a conversation with someone who claims to worship the God of the Bible who didn't agree that the Father is God. I think we almost have the opposite problem—most Christians seem to have a hard time *not* thinking of the Father (to the exclusion of the other members of the godhead) when we hear "God." Admit it—if I say, "In the beginning God created the heavens and the earth" about which member of the Trinity do you think? Hopefully by the time we're done studying the Trinity you'll recognize this for what it is—idolatry.[1]

THE HOLY SPIRIT IS GOD

Demonstrating that the Holy Spirit is God takes a little more work. The clearest passage that demonstrates the nature of the Holy Spirit is Acts 5:3, 4, where Peter at once says that Ananias has lied to the Holy Spirit but then turns right around and says, "You have not lied to men but to God." Peter obviously had no problems equating the Holy Spirit with God.

In Romans 8:9–11, especially verse 11, we see that the Holy Spirit raised Jesus from the dead. But in Acts 2:24 Peter, preaching under the influence of the Spirit, says that "God raised Him up again." There he goes again, confusing God with the Holy Spirit! But is he really confused?

Last, we looked at Exodus 17:2 wherein Moses asks the Israelites, "Why do you test the LORD [Hebrew: YHWH,

---

1   Idolatry in its essence is worship of anything or anyone that is not the God of Abraham, Isaac, and Jacob. If the object of our worship is not exactly identical to the God of the Bible, then we are worshiping something other than Him, and thus we commit idolatry, even if that object of worship has the same name.

Yahweh]?" But in Hebrews 3:9 we see that the Holy Spirit says about that same time, "Your fathers tried Me by testing Me." So apparently even the Holy Spirit thinks He is the Yahweh of the Old Testament! If Peter is confused about the nature of the Holy Spirit, then the Holy Spirit is equally confused, no?

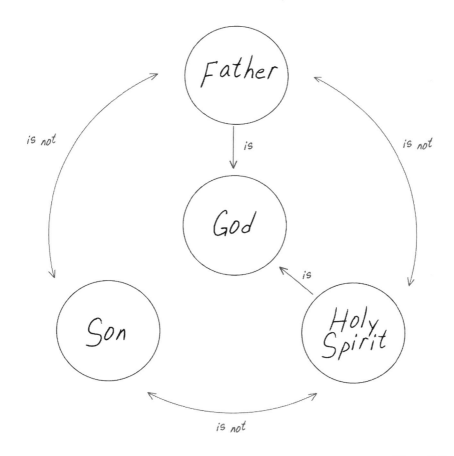

Figure 5-2

Jehovah's Witnesses argue that the Holy Spirit is "a controlled force that Jehovah God uses to accomplish a variety of his purposes...[which] can be likened to electricity, a force that can be adapted to perform a great variety of operations."[2] Mormons make a distinction between the "Holy Spirit" (God's presence via an essence)[3] and the "Holy Ghost" (the third god in the Mormon trinity).[4] But neither group really spends a lot of time talking about the Holy Spirit; their primary focus seems to be on trying to disprove that Jesus is fully God. Have you ever wondered why?

THE SON IS GOD

I took the kids to John 20:28, where we see, if the Jehovah's Witnesses are to be believed, Thomas cursing out of excitement.[5] But considering that "the LORD will not hold him guiltless who takes His name in vain" (Exodus 20:7; Deuteronomy 5:11, NKJV), is it reasonable to think that Thomas, a devout Jew, would do this—in front of Jesus no less? And if he did blaspheme like this, surely an orthodox rabbi would rebuke him, would he not? Yet Jesus did not.

---

2   *Should You Believe in the Trinity?* (Warwick, N.Y.: Watchtower Bible and Tract Society of Pennsylvania, 2006), 20.

3   "Holy Spirit," Mormon Research Ministry, accessed September 9, 2016, http://www.mrm.org/holy-spirit.

4   "Holy Ghost," Mormon Research Ministry, accessed September 9, 2016, http://www.mrm.org/holy-ghost.

5   This was an argument posited to me by my JW "bus buddy." I tell the story of those encounters in *Book 3: Practical Apologetics*. More official sources explain that it's okay to refer to Jesus as "God" (even with a capital "G") but that only Jehovah, to whom Jesus prayed in John 17:3, is "the only *true* God."

Why did I take the kids to this verse when I rejected another student's homework answer citing Martha's confession in John 11:27? Well, it's not what Thomas said that's interesting here—it's what Jesus said, or rather did *not* say, that's so amazing. Take a look at Acts 10:25, 26. There Cornelius falls at Peter's feet in an act of worship. What was Peter's response? "No way, dude. Get up before Jesus sees you!" Peter refused this man's worship because there is only One worthy of worship. Now turn to Revelation 19:10 and then 22:8, 9, where not once but *twice* the apostle John was so overwhelmed that he fell at the angel's feet and began to worship him; but both times the angel rebuked him and said, "Worship God and Him only!" So it's clear that a godly man like Peter knew he was not worthy of worship, and it's clear that angels know they are not worthy of worship. But not Jesus; Jesus accepted worship. Anyone who accepts worship like this must be, as C. S. Lewis so eloquently said, either Lord, a liar, or a lunatic— Jesus offers us no other option. He cannot be simply a "great moral teacher" because Jesus claimed to be God, accepted worship, and told people He was "the Truth"—the only way to the Father; great moral teachers don't flat-out lie about their identity and lead people to the pit of hell. And there's no evidence to point to that would suggest that Jesus was anything other than fully in His right mind.[6]

We then looked at Colossians 2:9, which tells us that in Jesus is the fullness of the Deity (i.e., He is "God in a bod"). Last, we noted how Colossians 1:15–20 says that all things were created

---

6   C. S. Lewis, *Mere Christianity* (New York: MacMillan Company, 1960), 56.

by Jesus and then referenced Genesis 1:1, which says that in the beginning *God* created. So either we have a contradiction on our hands or Jesus is God. Pick one.

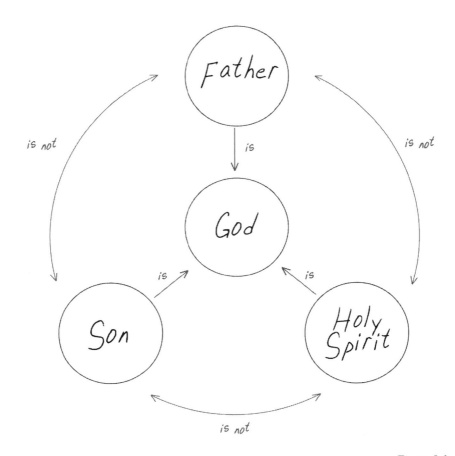

Figure 5-3

A CONTRADICTION?

So now we know that the Father is God, the Son is God, and the Holy Spirit is God. But in the previous lesson we learned that the Father is not the Son, the Son is not the Holy Spirit,

Chapter 5: The Trinity
Part 2: The "Is's"

and the Holy Spirit is not the Father; and to put the icing on the cake, somehow we have but *one* God. Doesn't this violate the law of noncontradiction?

Well, no. It doesn't.

If we were to say that we have one God and three Gods, then we would indeed have a contradiction on our hands — both statements cannot be true at the same time and in the same sense, no matter what kind of magic herbs your doctor prescribes for you. But that's not what I'm saying at all. What I'm saying is that we have one *God* manifest in three *Persons;* or, as others have said, "One *what* and three *whos.*"

ESSENCE AND ROLES

Have you ever wondered why we always say "Father, Son, and Holy Spirit" in that order? Is it because the Father is "more God" than the Son? Is the Holy Spirit somehow less God than the Son? One could argue that, but he'd be revealing a lack of understanding of the differences between essence and role.

Essence, in short, is who you *are*. Role is what you *do*. I warned the kids very strongly not to do what my former teammates did during my days playing basketball — they confused their essence with their role. If you were to ask them, "Who are you?" they'd invariably say, "I'm a basketball player." Big mistake; and it's a mistake that men especially make all the time as we find our sense of worth from our jobs. Want to find a miserable man? Find one who is unsatisfied with his job — one who works in an environment where he gets no respect and is not valued as an employee. Or find a workaholic who has recently lost his job and is "enjoying" a prolonged period of unemployment. When we confuse who we are with what we do, and then when what we do changes unexpectedly, a man will have serious emotional problems to deal with. When someone asks who you are, your answer as a Christian should be something more along the lines of "I'm a blood-bought and bullet-proof child of the King." It is in Christ that we find our identity and our sense of worth—not in the things we do.

SO WHAT ABOUT JOHN 10:30?

Now do you see what Jesus meant in John 10:30 when He said, "I and the Father are one"? Of course, He wasn't saying they are one in number, because we've already proven that the Father is not the Son and the Son is not the Father! The Mormons tell us that Jesus and the Father are "one in purpose"—like the Wonder Twins, I suppose—but if that were the case then the Pharisees wouldn't have sought to kill Him, because they considered themselves to be "one in purpose" with God— on His team and doing His will. No, what Jesus was talking about was His *essence*—He was saying "I and the Father are one in *essence*," or in plain English, "I'm God. How you like them apples?" According to Mosaic law, there were a number of offenses that warranted the death penalty, and blasphemy was one of them.[7] That Jesus claimed essential equality with God is evident by the reaction of the experts in the law that we see in verses 31–33.

---

7   Leviticus 24:14, 16, 23. Other capital offenses included, but were not limited to—murder (Exodus 21:12), rape (Deuteronomy 22:23–37), false prophecy (Deuteronomy 13:5), witchcraft (Exodus 22:18), adultery (Leviticus 20:10), homosexual acts (Leviticus 20:13), and kidnapping (Exodus 21:16).

Oh, and the Son of God thing? While I cannot be my own dad, my dad and I are both Krefts. So while I may not be Bruce Kreft, that does not make me any less "Krefty" than him.

AND NOW A WORD ABOUT MARRIAGE

The last thing a young Christian wife wants to hear is the "s" word: *submission*. The Bible calls women to submit to their husbands, and this can be really, really hard to swallow (it's part of the Curse, after all; see Genesis 3:16, cf. 4:7). But is the wife any less valuable in the eyes of God than the husband? No, absolutely not. Is the husband any more or less valuable than the wife in the eyes of God? No, of course not; both are His creation, and Christ died both for men and women alike. Man and woman are of the same essence.

When I said this, one of my students floored me with his insight. "Right, because they are *one flesh!*" Bingo, Yahtzee, praise-a-lujah! I'm right-handed, but that doesn't mean that the left side of my body is useless; for without the left side of my body, my right hand wouldn't have the strength to do what it does—I would simply fall over! The man and his wife are equal in *essence*, but both have very different *roles*. Men are terrible at being mommies, and women are terrible at being daddies. Neither was designed to replace the other, but rather the woman was given to the man to *complete* him. But here's the really hard part: while the man has been placed in the home as the head of the family unit, he is called to do so by— get this—dying to himself and putting his wife's needs above his own, the exact same way that Christ did for the Church! This is how you know that God has a sense of humor; He tells the one with the brain damage[8] that he has to lead by being a servant.

Why am I teaching your sixth-graders about marriage relationships? Because marriage is a picture of the Trinity, of course.

God never gives up his position as the head of the marriage relationship, so instead of "Father" at the top of the Trinity diagram, write "God." Now where the Son sits (at the right hand of the Father) in the diagram, write "Man"—because the man fulfills the role of Christ in the relationship—called to lead by being a servant and called to life by dying to himself. Finally, write "Wife" where the Holy Spirit sits in the diagram—it's her job to support her husband, to inspire him, and at times to remind him of what God has said (while at the same time trying to be careful not to *take over* the Holy Spirit's

---

8   I explained to the kids that at about six weeks after conception, a baby boy's brain is bathed in testosterone, which effectively severs most of the connections between the right and left sides of the brain (http://itre.cis.upenn.edu/~myl/languagelog/archives/003541.html)— which goes a long way to explaining why men take much longer to "get in touch" with their feelings. Our normal reaction to a traumatic event or an offense is anger, but after the right brain sends a carrier pigeon over to the left side (probably several such birds, since the left brain is busy shooting at them), we finally figure out in our internal caveman voice, "Me not angry. Me sad." Women, on the other hand, are typically much more in tune with what they feel and have little trouble articulating this. This brain damage is why men are like waffles and women are like spaghetti—two men can beat the tar out of each other on a court, field or ring and then go out and have dinner together as if nothing ever happened—we compartmentalize quite easily (brain damage has its upsides!) Women, on the other hand, well, it isn't like that at all. Every piece seems to touch every other piece—it's a full-brain experience, which frankly sounds scary to me.

job—a delicate balance for sure). Have you ever noticed that it's usually the women in a marriage who come to Christ first? Many churches have more women in attendance than men, which I think indicates a greater sensitivity to the Holy Spirit's leading.

If you've never thought about the parallels between a married couple and the triune godhead, maybe now you'll understand a little better why God places such a high premium on marriage and why He states very bluntly, "I *hate* divorce" (Malachi 2:16, italics added). Why does He hate it so much? Because it debases the very nature of God and grossly misrepresents His relationship with Himself to an unbelieving world. Is not a good name rather to be chosen than great riches (Proverbs 22:1)? How much more valuable, then, is the name and character of God than all the riches this world can offer? I have much more to say about this, but that's for another book.

You represent the God of the universe on this earth. Are you representing Him well?

WHY ALL THE FUSS OVER JESUS?

So why is it that with all the arguments about God, people seem to get the most up in arms about the second member of the Trinity? We can say "God" in public, and we can pray to "God" but why is it that military chaplains are told they can't pray in Jesus' name?[9] Why is it that entertainers can thank "God" at a secular music awards festival and nobody bats an

---

9   Bob Unruh, "Chaplain Who Prayed 'In Jesus' Name' Sues Over Dismissal," accessed September 9, 2016, http://www.wnd.com/2011/11/365689/.

eye,[10] but when a football player is an outspoken Christian and unafraid to talk about Jesus, he gets lambasted by the secular media?[11]

HOMEWORK

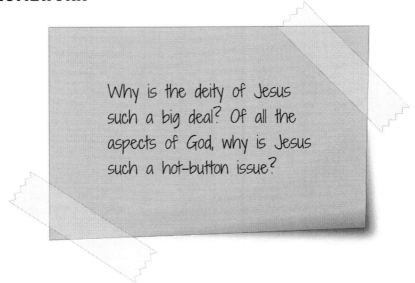

Why is the deity of Jesus such a big deal? Of all the aspects of God, why is Jesus such a hot-button issue?

10   "30 Stars Thank God for Their Grammys in 60 Seconds," YouTube video, 1:05, posted by "AOL Entertainment," October 12, 2012, https://www.youtube.com/watch?v=jcgYcDsTFmI.

11   Jen Floyd Engel, "Why the heck do we hate Tim Tebow?" Fox Sports, accessed September 9, 2016, http://www.foxsports.com/nfl/story/Tim-Tebow-why-the-heck-do-we-hate-him-110211.

The Trinity

*Part 3: Why Is the Deity of Jesus
Such a Big Deal?*

T O GET THE CONVERSATION GOING, I ASKED
the kids, "What's *the* most important question Jesus ever asked?" They immediately went catatonic. It was almost scary how quiet the room got. So I broke the silence with some seed questions to get their brains going "Was it 'What's for dinner?' or maybe 'Where's the bathroom?'" Okay, it wasn't to get their brains going—it was to get them to make some noise. Silence like that is painful.

I don't have any of their guesses written down, but after fielding some failed attempts, I had them all turn to and read Matthew 16:13–17. The most important question Jesus ever asked was "Who do you say that I am?" That's a bold claim for me to make, but I think it's the most important question for a very good reason—and this reason is the answer to the homework question from last week.

We turned to John 8:24 and read the words of Christ: "Unless you believe that I am He, you will die in your sins."

"BUT MY BIBLE SAYS SOMETHING DIFFERENT"

The 2011 NIV says, "If you do not believe that I am He..." The 1984 NIV says "that I am [the one I claim to be]..." (bracketed wording theirs). The KJV has "that I am *he*..." and the NASB says "that I am *He*..." (italics theirs in both). What's with the brackets and italics? Those are devices used by the respective translators of each version to indicate that the word or phrase so decorated is not in the original language but was added to make the English read like, well, like English. So Jesus did not say, "that I am he..." ("he" who?), but rather, in Greek He said ἐγώ εἰμί (*ego eimi*), which literally translated means "I am." We see this construct used again in verse 28, but when Jesus uses it again in 8:58, he gets a violent reaction from his audience. What was that reaction? In verse 59 they all bought tickets to a rock concert. Why would they do such a thing?

The reason is simple: Jesus' Jewish audience understood that He was using the same language that the Greek translation of the Old Testament used in Exodus 3:14, where God told Moses to tell them that "I AM" sent him. In Hebrew, that "I AM" is יהוה, which, when transliterated into English, is "YHWH." You may have heard this name in English as "Yahweh" (or "Jehovah" if you go through Latin before getting to English). In Greek, though, it is simply *ego eimi*. It is the sacred covenant name of God, and to use it in the manner Jesus did was to claim equality, nay, *identity* with God Himself. In their eyes

He committed blasphemy, which was one of the few capital offenses under Jewish law.[1]

But that still doesn't plainly answer the question "Why do so many people argue about who Jesus is?" It only tells us that Jesus made a pretty extraordinary claim—that He is YHWH; but we're getting closer. Hang in there.

WE'VE GOT A PROBLEM

The Bible tells us that we were all born dead (Psalm 51:5; Ephesians 2:1)—physically alive, for sure, but spiritually deader than a doornail. Left to our own devices, this is a hopeless situation for us because just as no man can grab himself by the ankles and hoist himself to the ceiling, no man can save himself from his own sinful condition and the eternal damnation that awaits him by default (John 3:36). He needs a savior—someone to rescue him. But who can possibly do this? Who can pay an infinite debt owed to an eternal God?

LET'S TAKE A LITTLE TRIP

To lay a truly solid foundation for our answer, I took the kids on a trip through the Bible. Here's the train of verses we studied[2]:

1. Isaiah 43:3, 11; 49:26; 60:16

2. Hosea 13:4

---

1   Leviticus 24:16

2   There is a longer, more detailed train of verses in *Book 3: Practical Apologetics*.

3. Luke 2:11

4. John 4:42

5. Acts 5:31; 13:23

6. 2 Timothy 1:10

7. Titus 1:4; 2:10, 13; 3:4, 6

8. 2 Peter 1:1, 11; 2:20; 3:2, 18

We can summarize this train of verses with the following syllogism:

Only YHWH can save man from his sin

Jesus is YHWH

Therefore, only Jesus can save man from his sin.

SO IF THE BIBLE IS SO CLEAR, WHY DO PEOPLE ARGUE SO MUCH ABOUT WHO JESUS IS?

Why is there so much argument about who Jesus is? Good question, but I think it's more helpful to ask a different question: "Where do these arguments about Jesus' identity come from?"

I'll give you a hint:

> *Our struggle is not against flesh and blood, but against the rulers, against the powers, against the world forces of this darkness, against the spiritual forces of wickedness in the heavenly places.* (Ephesians 6:12)

> *Even if our gospel is veiled, it is veiled to those who are perishing, in whose case the god of this world has blinded the minds of the unbelieving so that they might not see the light of the gospel of the glory of Christ, who is the image of God.* (2 Corinthians 4:3, 4)

The battle we engage in when we connect with people from other faiths—people who deny the essential deity of Christ, deny that there is but *one* God, and deny that the only way to be saved is solely through the grace of God (*not* by works, lest any man should boast)—is not a physical battle. Rather, it is spiritual and mental.

Consider what else is written about the enemy of our souls:

> *Be of sober spirit, be on the alert. Your adversary, the devil, prowls around like a roaring lion, seeking someone to devour.* (1 Peter 5:8)

> *You are of your father the devil, and you want to do the desires of your father. He was a murderer from the beginning, and does not stand in the truth because there is no truth in him. Whenever he speaks a lie, he speaks from his own nature, for he is a liar and the father of lies.* (John 8:44)

Satan has been lying about what God has said since he appeared on the scene all the way back in Genesis 3: "Has God *really* said...?" He perverts the Word of God by adding to it, removing from it, and quoting it out of context to suit his purposes. Getting people to think they're following the real Jesus Christ when in fact they're following a fraud is perhaps his greatest achievement.

OKAY, FINE. SO THE DEVIL'S BEHIND ALL THIS. BUT WHY?

Why do people argue so much about who Jesus is? Why is who He is such a big deal? Because who you say Jesus is is the solitary pivot on which your eternal destination is balanced. If you get the answer to that question wrong, no matter how wonderful a life you think you've lived, you will spend an eternity separated from God in a very real place called hell.

> *"Not everyone who says to Me, 'Lord, Lord,' will enter the kingdom of heaven, but he who does the will of My Father who is in heaven will enter. Many will say to Me on that day, 'Lord, Lord, did we not prophesy in Your name, and in Your name cast out demons, and in Your name perform many miracles?' And then I will declare to them, 'I never knew you; depart from Me, you who practice lawlessness.'"* (Matthew 7:21–23)

Make sure you've got the right Jesus.

HOMEWORK

In the next lesson we'll take a little closer look at the Holy Spirit, specifically His *personhood*. The assignment for this week is to answer the following question:

What is a "person"?

7 The Holy Spirit Is a "Person"

W E OFTEN HEAR THE CHRISTIAN CLICHÉ "one God in three persons," but how often do we actually stop and think about what it means to be a person? When I asked the kids this, I saw them transform from bright-eyed students into deer caught in the headlights of an oncoming teacher. So I backed up a bit and asked them a question or two to get their gears engaged.

"Is a dog a person?" I queried.

"No."

"Why not?"

"Because it can't talk."

"Oh, okay, so because my six-month-old daughter can't talk, she's not a person? What if someone has laryngitis—does he lose his personhood?"

"No, that's not what we mean."

"Okay, so what, then, does it mean to be a 'person'?"

"People wear clothes."

"Did you shower this morning?"

"Yes."

"Did you wear your clothes in the shower?"

"No."

"Did you stop being a person when you took your clothes off?"

The point was well-taken by the class—there's more to being a person than the things we do or the things we drape over our respective bodies. After more pressing and prodding on my part, we eventually stumbled onto three basic characteristics that define a person: emotions, intellect, and will.[1]

1. **Emotions**: when the IBM super computer "Deep Blue" lost to world champion chess player Gary Kasparov 2–4 in February 1996, that computer "felt" the same as it did after it was upgraded and

---

1   Paul Enns, *The Moody Handbook of Theology* (Chicago: Moody Press, 1989), 245.

beat Kasparov 3½ to 2½ a year later. Kasparov, I'm sure, did not feel the same after each match. He has emotions, Deep Blue does not.

2. **Intellect**: the ability to think and reason sets us apart from animals. Computers and animals react to stimuli, but human beings can be proactive (when they're not overcome with laziness)

3. **Will**: we have the power to choose our own actions and to determine what and how to get that which we desire or to avoid that which we detest.

The Jehovah's Witnesses assert (rather vociferously, in my experience) that the Holy Spirit is God's "active force"[2]— sort of like radio waves, a magnetic field, gravity, or a tractor beam. According to the JWs, the Holy Spirit is just how God gets stuff done. But is this true? Since the only things true about God is what He says about Himself, I submit to you that that would be the best place to start. Let's see if the Holy Spirit is depicted as having emotions, intellect, and a will of His own.

THE HOLY SPIRIT HAS EMOTIONS

In Ephesians 4:30 we learn that the Holy Spirit can be *grieved*. The Greek word translated "grieve" in this verse (λυπεῖτε) is the same word used in Matthew 26:37 in discussing how Jesus felt in His spirit in the Garden of Gethsemane before He was arrested. Jesus felt gut-wrenching anguish—the same gut-

---

2   *Should You Believe in the Trinity?* (Warwick, N.Y.: Watchtower Bible and Tract Society of Pennsylvania, 2006), 20.

wrenching anguish that the Holy Spirit is said to feel when we sin against each other.

In Romans 15:30, we learn that the Holy Spirit *loves*—not that He transmits love, as we might expect an impersonal force to do—but that He Himself loves.

Hebrews 10:29 demonstrates that the Holy Spirit can be *insulted*, which cannot be done to an impersonal "active force." When was the last time you saw a magnet get offended?

THE HOLY SPIRIT HAS INTELLECT

Intellect is simply the ability to reason or to think rational thoughts. One might also slip "self-awareness" in here. Intellect is what allows us to learn from other people's mistakes as well as our own. It allows us to apply abstract concepts to concrete phenomena. Does the Holy Spirit, as depicted in the Bible, demonstrate intellect? Well, let's take a quick look.

In Acts 13:2; Mark 13:11; Acts 1:16, 21:11; John 16:13; and Hebrews 3:7 we see that the Holy Spirit Himself *speaks*.

John 16:13 also shows the Holy Spirit having the ability to *hear* and *guide*.

In John 14:26; Luke 12:12; Hebrews 9:8; 1 Corinthians 2:13; and Acts 1:2 the Holy Spirit *teaches*.

He *counsels* in John 14:15–17.

He is said to *know the future* in Acts 21:11.

He *prays* for us in Romans 8:26.

And in my favorite passage on the personality and deity of the Holy Spirit, Acts 5:3–5, we see Him being *lied to*. A lie cannot be told to an impersonal force.

THE HOLY SPIRIT HAS WILL

An impersonal force can have no will of its own, for it cannot desire anything—it just *is*. So if we see any evidence of the Holy Spirit having a will of His own, surely this would disqualify Him as an impersonal "it," no?

In 1 Corinthians 12 we see that the Holy Spirit Himself is responsible for *giving* spiritual gifts to believers. In verse 11 we see that He gives these gifts of His *own will*.

Acts 20:28 shows that the Holy Spirit Himself *appoints* overseers in the Church. It's not the Father working via the Holy Spirit.

The Holy Spirit can be *resisted* (as in stubbornly refusing to do His will), as seen in Acts 7:51.

And in Acts 13:4 we see the Holy Spirit *sending* Barnabas and Saul out, not forcing them out.

HOMEWORK

In the next lesson we're going to change gears a bit and move into practical apologetics. Now that we know we have good reasons to believe the Bible, and now that we know a bit more about its Author, we're going to see how this looks in everyday life. To that end I assign the following:

Go to YouTube and watch a video titled "The Math of the Great Flood" (http://www.youtube.com/watch?v=5svTzxVa-xQ).

If by the time you read this the video is no longer available, use your favorite search engine and search for "math great flood" and read the arguments skeptics commonly make against Noah's flood.

You'll find the discussion of this question in *"Jesus" Is Not the Answer to Every Sunday School Question, Book 3: Practical Apologetics.*

Appendix
Recommended Resources

My mom says I've always liked to argue,[3] so I guess you could say that I've been an apologist-in-training since I was a little boy. But after having my first encounter with an atheist over a book review on Amazon.com, I decided it was time to get serious about learning how to talk to people with whom I disagreed. Many of my favorite resources can be found in the footnotes of this book, but the following are other volumes that I have not cited that were instrumental in forming a solid apologetic foundation.

THEOLOGY

The Holy Bible. I really hope this goes without saying, but if you want to deepen your understanding of God, you have to spend time with Him, not sit at the feet of others who do.

Knowledge of the Holy, The Pursuit of God, and *The Attributes of God,* by A. W. Tozer. Actually, you pretty much can't go wrong with any of A. W. Tozer's books.

Mere Christianity, by C. S. Lewis.

More Than a Carpenter, by Josh and Sean McDowell.

---

3   I don't agree, of course.

REFERENCE BOOKS

The New Evidence That Demands a Verdict, by Josh McDowell. This is an absolute must-have.

LOGIC

Come, Let Us Reason: An Introduction to Logical Thinking, by Norman L. Geisler and Ronald M. Brooks. This was actually the very first book I read on logic, and it really lit my fire for the topic.

Socratic Logic: A Logic Text Using Socratic Method, Platonic Questions, and Aristotelian Principles, by Peter Kreeft. This is a serious text that I would say is at least high school-level. It is extremely rigorous and contains problems to work through at the end of every chapter.

Introductory Logic, by James B. Nance. This is a full-on curriculum that our firstborn took as an online class with the author twice a week. It's not cheap, but it's worth every penny.

Made in the USA
Middletown, DE
14 March 2019